Debbie MacKinnon trained as a medical and scientific illustrator at Hornsey College. After working in a design studio, she became art director at Dorling Kindersley and then at Frances Lincoln. Currently a freelance designer and writer, her previous books with Anthea Sieveking include the very popular Right Start series: *How Many? What Am I? What's Inside? What Colour? What Noise? What Shape?* and *What Size?* as well as other titles such as *My First ABC, The Seasons, Eye Spy Colours* and most recently the I can Do It! series: *Let's Play* and *My Day*, all for Frances Lincoln.

Anthea Sieveking has worked as a photographer in London for many years. After studying photography at Oxford School of Art, she set up a studio specialising in pictures of actors and writers. She went on to become a well-known photographer of young children and babies. Her books include *Your Child's Development, The Baby's Book of Babies* (with Kathy Henderson), the Nursery Rhyme Board Books, the Right Start series, *Baby's First Year* and many other titles with Debbie MacKinnon (listed above), all published by Frances Lincoln.

for Dora and Jack – D.M.
for Alan – A.S.

all about ME copyright © Frances Lincoln Limited 1994
Text copyright © Debbie MacKinnon 1994
Illustrations copyright © Anthea Sieveking 1994

First published in Great Britain in 1994 by
Frances Lincoln Limited, 4 Torriano Mews
Torriano Avenue, London NW5 2RZ

First paperback edition 1996

British Library Cataloguing in Publication Data
available on request

ISBN 0-7112-0861-1   hardback
ISBN 0-7112-1100-0   paperback

Design and art direction Debbie MacKinnon
Set in Futura Book
Printed in Hong Kong

3 5 7 9 8 6 4 2

all about
ME

Debbie MacKinnon
Photographs by Anthea Sieveking

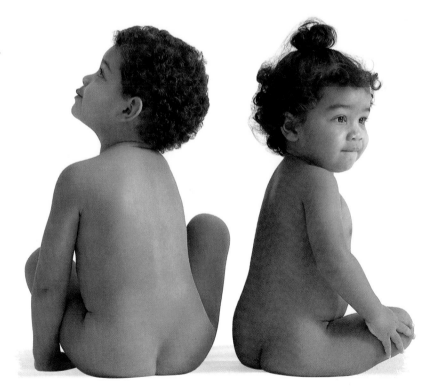

FRANCES LINCOLN

My body

Can you stretch right out like Kelly?

Now point to all the parts of her body.

- head
- back
- shoulder
- chest
- arm
- leg
- tummy
- hair
- knee
- bottom
- fingers
- toes
- face
- wrist
- ankle
- hand
- foot
- elbow
- eye
- nose
- mouth

Can you find all these on your own body?

My face

Can you point to all these parts?
• eyes • ears • mouth • nose
• eyelashes • eyebrows
• lips • teeth • chin
• cheeks • forehead

My hair

Isabel has fair, curly hair.

Rosie has long, thick hair.

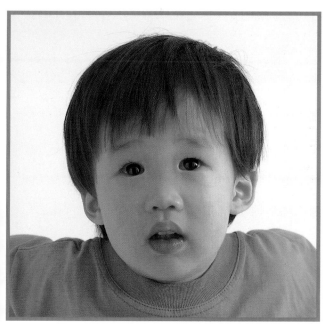

Christopher has dark, straight hair.

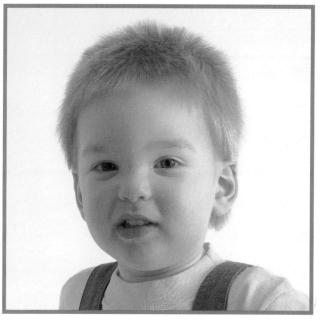

Joshua has short, spiky hair.

What kind of hair do you have?

My hands

Are your hands as big as Hannah's?
Put your hands on top of hers. Now
count your fingers.

Christopher needs both hands to pick up big teddy.

Jim likes pressing the buttons on the phone with his finger.

Elliot holds out his hand to catch the bubble.

Levi picks up a pea with his finger and thumb.

What else can you do with your hands?

My feet

Can you stretch forward
and touch your feet?
Jack can almost reach his.

You have two feet and
ten toes. Point to your big
toe and your littlest toe.
Now wiggle all your toes!

Kelly balances
on tip-toe.

Ann walks along
the plank, without
falling off!

Katherine pushes
with her feet,
and scoots
along on
her trike.

Rosie jumps up and
down on the trampoline.

What else can you do with your feet?

My ears, eyes, nose and mouth

Joshua likes cooking. Here he is calling Laura to come and try a freshly baked biscuit.

Laura can hear Joshua with her ears.

Laura can see the biscuit with her eyes.

Now she can smell it with her nose,

and she can taste the biscuit with her tongue. Yummy!

Careful, it might still be hot!

What else do you like to taste?

My skin

Your skin covers your whole body. Daniel has fallen over, and grazed his knees. Now he has two plasters while he waits for new skin to grow underneath. Daniel likes his plasters!

You can touch and feel with your skin.

Levi's new jersey feels rough and scratchy.

Christopher's rabbit feels soft and furry.

Jessica's ball feels
smooth and round.

The water in Isabel's
pool feels cold and wet...

...but Isabel's towel
feels warm and dry.

Touch Mummy's face.
Now touch Daddy's face.
How do they feel?

Looking after my body

Your body gets dirty every day.

Mark has found his big sister's chocolate, so he really needs a good wash!

It's bathtime...

Now Mark is clean again and Kelly is having a hairwash. Can you wash yourself?

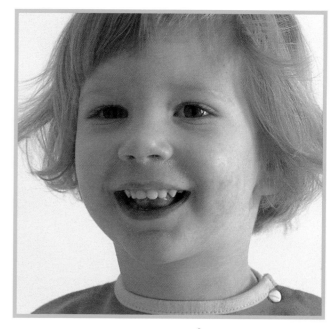

Teeth need cleaning too –
Ann is brushing hers.

Now Ann's teeth are
white and shiny.

Mummy is cutting Jack's fingernails.
Snip, snip, snip – it doesn't hurt.
Don't forget the toenails!

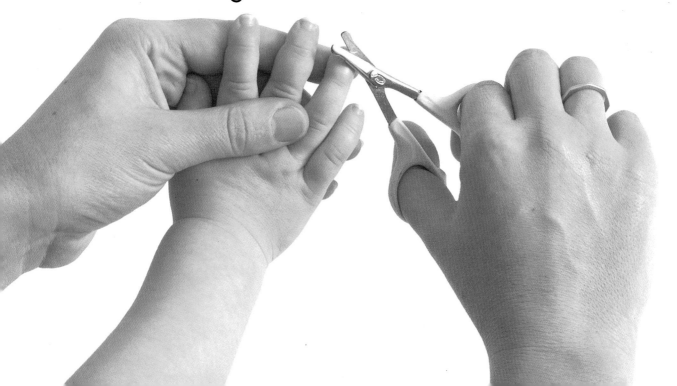

How many?

What a lot of parts in your body.
Can you count them all?

1 head • tummy • nose • mouth • tongue • neck

2 eyes • ears • arms • hands • legs • feet • cheeks

10 fingers • toes • fingernails • toenails

20 teeth (have you got them all yet?)

and don't forget **1,000s** of hairs on your head!

MORE BOOKS IN PAPERBACK BY DEBBIE MACKINNON AND ANTHEA SIEVEKING FROM FRANCES LINCOLN

MY FIRST ABC

From Abby's apple to Zack's Zebra, this lively ABC of toddlers with bright, beautiful photographs, is perfect for the very young. An enjoyable way to learn the alphabet.

Suitable for Nursery Level

ISBN 0-7112-0897-2 £4.99

THE SEASONS

This colourful photographic book covers the whole year from the first buds of spring right through to a winter field.

Suitable for Nursery Level

ISBN 0-7112-0909-X £4.99

THE RIGHT START SERIES

Lively text accompanies bright photographs in this fun series of early concept books for toddlers.

Suitable for Nursery Education and Early Years Education.

How Many? ISBN 0-7112-0802-6 £3.99
What Noise? ISBN 0-7112-1138-8 £3.99
What Shape? ISBN 0-7112-1302-X £3.99
What Am I? ISBN 0-7112-1276-7 £4.99
What's Inside? ISBN 0-7112-1054-3 £3.99
What Colour? ISBN 0-7112-1068-3 £4.99
What Size? ISBN 0-7112-1336-4 £4.99

Frances Lincoln titles are available from all good bookshops.
Prices are correct at time of printing, but may be subject to change.